Fo

HELLFIGHTERS OPERATIONS MANUAL 3

The Conflict
of a Hellfighter

HELLFIGHTERS OPERATIONS MANUAL 3

The Conflict of a Hellfighter

RICHARD W. HEADRICK

HELLFIGHTER PUBLICATIONS

FINALLY, MY BRETHREN, BE STRONG IN THE LORD, AND IN THE POWER OF HIS MIGHT. PUT ON THE WHOLE ARMOUR OF GOD, THAT YE MAY BE ABLE TO STAND AGAINST THE WILES OF THE DEVIL. FOR WE WRESTLE NOT AGAINST FLESH AND BLOOD, BUT AGAINST PRINCIPALITIES, AGAINST POWERS, AGAINST THE RULERS OF THE DARKNESS OF THIS WORLD, AGAINST SPIRITUAL WICKEDNESS IN HIGH PLACES. WHEREFORE TAKE UNTO YOU THE WHOLE ARMOUR OF GOD, THAT YE MAY BE ABLE TO WITHSTAND IN THE EVIL DAY, AND HAVING DONE ALL, TO STAND.

EPHESIANS 6:10-13

The Cover

The Conflict of a Hellfighter describes the life of a modern-day warrior. Those with an allegiance to fight spiritual battles and stand against the legions of evil are among an elite band of soldiers. This army is responsible for driving back Satan's frontline forces and for protecting our brothers and sisters from the world's most powerful enemy.

Our armor, unlike the helmet depicted on the cover of this book, is not a physical armor, but rather a spiritual armor made available through our submission to our Commander and Chief,

Jesus Christ. No blade can pierce it. No enemy can destroy it. Join God's army of Hellfighters today and become an unstoppable warrior in the greatest conflict in history. Victory is guaranteed!

Appreciation

To Lynn Lyon,
my sister-in-law and
executive assistant,
an exceptional lady, loyal wife and
extraordinary mother.

Dedication

This book is dedicated
to my beloved wife, Gina.
She is a faithful and loyal lover of
my foolishness, a steadfast and valiant
servant of the Lord Jesus Christ,
an exceptional lady and supportive
companion. Fearless, yet compassionate,
she's my foxhole buddy to the end.
I love you, my sweet precious.

Contents

HE AROSE, AND
SMOTE THE
PHILISTINES
UNTIL HIS HAND
WAS WEARY,
AND HIS HAND
CLAVE UNTO
THE SWORD:
AND THE LORD
WROUGHT A
GREAT VICTORY
THAT DAY…

2 SAMUEL 23:10A

Introduction

All my life I have been fascinated with knives and bladed weapons of all sorts, especially swords. And it has always intrigued me how a man can take a worthless piece of steel and carefully shape and temper it into a thing of beauty and purpose.

Human life is similar in some ways to a piece of steel. Each person has the potential to become something great. However, the decisions we make and the role we allow God to play in our lives determine what shape our lives take.

Wouldn't it be a disgrace to see the world's greatest sword maker take a big, impressive piece of steel, worthy of becoming the most beautiful sword ever made, and waste it by making nothing more than a common pocketknife out of it? A pocketknife seems so small and insignificant doesn't it?

Just like a pocketknife, some men will never accomplish much of anything. Why? Because they fail to apply themselves to the purpose God has for them and, as a result, just waste away. They refuse the expert craftsmanship of their Creator who desires to shape them into a one-of-a-kind masterpiece.

True enough, a pocketknife of any size is good for some things: trimming fingernails, carving a small piece of wood, cutting tape from a package, etc. But, even though pocketknives serve certain purposes, I've never seen a movie or read a story in which a pocketknife was the center of attention, have you?

When I was a young man, I remember seeing the movie *The Alamo*, starring John Wayne. In the movie, one of the main characters was Jim Bowie, creator of the famed "Bowie knife." Jim's "Bowie knife" had a huge fixed blade which, when pulled from its sheath, assured the enemy they were facing a determined man with a formidable weapon. I'm sure the other 188 men who died at the Alamo in San Antonio, Texas back in 1836 had pocketknives, but not one of their pocketknives, nor Jim's pocketknife for that matter, made the history books, yet Jim's "Bowie knife" did.

A pocketknife just doesn't have much pizzazz does it? And to be honest, most Christians don't have much pizzazz either. Do you know why? Because the faith of most Christians is about the size of a puny, little pocketknife.

In most instances, when you read about Biblical heroes, swords, not pocketknives, play some kind of role in *helping* them make it to the history books.

This book, the third in this series of *Hellfighters Operations Manuals*, entitled *The Conflict of a Hellfighter*, measures the progression of a Christian's faith from the day of his spiritual birth and Biblical infancy to his induction into the Hellfighters Hall of Fame.

To trace these milestones of faith in a Christian's walk with Christ, we will use the analogy that your faith in Christ is a bladed weapon and the size and strength of that weapon is dependent upon your level of commitment to Christ.

A Christian's walk with Christ begins with Pocketknife-sized Faith that has the potential to grow; however, it will only grow at the same rate in which you study and obey God's Word.

The Bible says in Romans 10:17, *...faith cometh by hearing, and hearing by the Word of God*, but James 1:22a says, *Be ye doers of the Word, and not hearers only...* In other words, puny, immature, Pocketknife-sized Faith will never amount to a hill of beans for Jesus, nor will any battles against the evil one be won unless you study God's Word and live it by example, as we all are commanded to do.

2 Timothy 2:15 reminds us, *Study to shew thyself approved unto God, a workman that needeth not to be ashamed, rightly dividing the Word of truth.* It makes sense that the more we study God's Word, the more we pray, the more we fellowship with Believers, and the more we endeavor to please

our Heavenly Father, the more our faith, courage and commitment to Jesus Christ will grow.

The more faith you possess and the more knowledge you gain, the more courage you will have and the more enthusiasm you will outwardly show for the cause of Jesus Christ.

The more powerful your faith becomes, the more dedicated and steadfast *you* will become. As you selflessly dedicate yourself to the study of God's Word and the fulfillment of its teachings, your immature faith will, in time, grow into a battle-ready Sword of Victory that can only be wielded by a champion of the faith, a true Hellfighter.

Uncompromised faith is a formidable weapon. It is the greatest weapon you possess in your fight against the hordes of Satan's seducing demons. The assurance of and your commitment to your faith determines the size and power of this most incredible weapon. So, think with me for a minute, does your faith still compare to the size of a pocketknife? Or is your faith already growing into a weapon comparable to that of a sword which you might possibly use to change the course of Christian history?

As you embark upon your journey to change the world for Christ, Jesus wants to assure you that, *...greater is He that is in you, than he that is in the world* (1 John 4:4b).

Everything you need to be victorious over Satan can be found within the pages of God's Word. So what are you waiting for, Hellfighter? Let's put on the whole armor of God and prepare for *The Conflict!*

LIFE IS A TEST.
IF YOU FAIL, IT'S HELL!

THEY SHALL BE
LIKE MIGHTY MEN,
WHO TREAD DOWN
THEIR ENEMIES IN
THE MIRE OF THE
STREETS IN THE
BATTLE. THEY SHALL
FIGHT BECAUSE
THE LORD IS WITH
THEM.

ZECHARIAH 10:5 (NKJV)

CHAPTER 1

What is a Hellfighter?

 irst of all, I'd like to ask you a question. Have you read any of our other *Hellfighters Operations Manuals*? If you have, you know what a Hellfighter is. If you haven't, then let me tell you.

Your initial thought may be that a Hellfighter is a man who fights raging oil well fires in some God-forsaken region of our globe. That's close! But, incorrect!

Around the world, God's Hellfighters are those who fight not only the visible effects of hell's raging inferno, but also the keeper of hell himself – Satan, the chief ruler of darkness. Ephesians 6:12 warns us who our opponents are when it says, *For we wrestle not against flesh and blood, but against principalities, against powers, against the rulers of the darkness of this world, against spiritual wickedness in high places.*

Your question to me may be, "How can mere mortals fight Satan and opponents such as these?" Well, that's an excellent question, and one that deserves an answer.

First of all, you must refuse to give him any kind of foothold in your life. You can deny him that right by refusing to participate in any of his clever enticements that, in appearance, have the allure of gold, the sweetness of candy, the sensuality of a maiden, the beauty of a flower and the promise of unequaled pleasures.

But, you can't win these victories unless you are well grounded in God's Word. Without faith and lots of it, Satan will deceive you, cause you to betray your Heavenly Father and ruin your testimony.

The Bible says in James 4:7b, ...*Resist the devil, and he will flee from you.* So don't believe Satan's lie from hell that says you're too weak to resist! Believe the truth that is recorded in 1 John 4:4b which says ...*greater is He that is in you, than he that is in the world.*

You may be wondering why anyone would ever want or need to fight Satan. Surely, he's just a figment of man's imagination, isn't he? NO! HE'S THE ESSENCE OF PURE EVIL.

When you investigate this deceiver, you will find that he not only exists, but that he is a liar, a cheat, a portrayer of untruths and a counterfeiter of all that is holy and righteous in the sight of God and man. Satan is, without question, the master artist of deception.

Just as a mirage seduces men of thirst, Satan seduces every man, woman, boy or girl who partakes of his delicacies. As a mirage holds empty promises, so do Satan's seductive pleasures. He will promise you everything but in the end, he will give you nothing; just like a mirage.

The good news is, it's not impossible for you or anyone else to resist Satan's deceptive tactics. On the contrary, it is *imperative*, for your well-being, that you resist them. The Bible tells us in Hebrews 11:25 that Moses did just that, *Choosing rather to suffer affliction with the people of God, than to enjoy the pleasures of sin for a season*; and because he was found faithful, God used Moses to accomplish great and mighty things for Him. Consequently, Moses went down in the history books as one of God's greatest Hellfighters.

Satan wants to trick you and everyone else into disbelieving the promises that God has for us. 2 Peter 1:4a tells us, *Whereby are given unto us exceeding great and precious promises...* If you belong to God and acknowledge His Son, Jesus, as your Lord and Savior, then your life need not be one of chaos and confusion. 1 Corinthians 14:33 tells us, *For God is not the author of confusion, but of peace...*

To become a Hellfighter, mediocre Christians must give up the lifestyle of this world and turn their backs on sin. You, and others like you, must commit your time, talents and resources to fulfill the great commission found in Matthew 28:19, 20 (NKJV): *"Go therefore and make disciples of all nations, baptizing them in the name of the Father and of the Son and of the Holy Spirit, teaching them to observe all things that I have commanded you; and lo, I am with you always, even to the end of the age." Amen.*

To sum it up, we Hellfighters are a league of extraordinary ladies and gentlemen who are bold enough to love the Lord our God with all our hearts, all our souls, all our minds, and all our strength.

Do you love Him that much? If so, why not become a Hellfighter and join us in doing great and mighty things for God? If you're already a Hellfighter, what are you waiting for? LET'S GO GETTUM!

LIFE IS A TEST.
IF YOU FAIL, IT'S HELL!

NOTE FROM THE AUTHOR:

As you read on, think seriously about where you stand with Jesus. I have written this book primarily for Believers. But, before we go any further, let me ask you a most important question. Are you a Believer in Jesus Christ? If not, read on anyway, friend. You may not understand anything at all about the Bible, but I promise this little book will help you understand your need for Jesus. That's the first step in getting on the right path. It's also your first step toward becoming a Hellfighter.

...Shout; for the Lord hath given you the city.

Joshua 6:16b

CHAPTER 2

The Victory is Up to Us

 n a world where wrong seems right, God has chosen a select few of us to battle valiantly against the realm of Heaven's archenemy, Satan.

After Satan rebelled against God and the kingdom of Heaven, he made his home in the bowels of the earth. As time passed and God placed man upon this sphere of dirt, Satan ventured out of his cankered domain and onto the surface of the earth and into the air above.

1 Peter 5:8b (NKJV) warns us that our ...*adversary the devil walks about like a roaring lion, seeking whom he may devour.* Ephesians 6:12 confirms to us that, *we wrestle not against flesh and blood, but against principalities, against powers, against the rulers of the darkness of this world, against spiritual wickedness in high places.*

Since the dawn of man, Satan has tried relentlessly to dim the light of God's glory. For thousands of years, God's angels, as well as His earthly warriors, have displayed gallant efforts to subdue Satan and confine his terror to the fiery bowels of the earth called hell.

The Bible tells us in Matthew 25:41b that hell is a place of ...*everlasting fire, prepared for the devil and his angels.* Mark 9:44 reveals that hell is, *Where their worm dieth not, and the fire is not quenched.* Matthew 13:50b mourns the fact that in hell, ...*there shall be wailing and gnashing of teeth.* Sounds like a place I don't want to get near, much less spend an eternity. What about you? The Bible also says that hell is a place of tormented souls. In Luke 16:24, Jesus tells us of a man who is in hell, *And he cried and said, Father Abraham, have mercy on me, and send Lazarus, that he may dip the tip of his finger in water, and cool my tongue; for I am tormented in this flame.*

God allows each of us to have a "freewill." This freewill lets us decide who we will serve: God or Satan. The majority, it seems, has decided to follow Satan. Why? Because he is the master deceiver. As a matter of fact, God allows this liar to coerce, deceive and recruit into his service any member of the human race who will not resist his temptations. Satan is truly the master artist of deception and the father of lies. His whole purpose for existence is to discredit God and corrupt you. But you can prevent him from doing so if you're willing to join the fight against evil and follow Jesus as a Hellfighter.

Satan paints a beautiful picture of all that he promises to do for you, but God's Word reveals that Satan is a liar and the truth is not in him. John 8:44b says, *…When he* [the devil] *speaketh a lie, he speaketh of his own: for he is a liar, and the father of it.*

Satan is a bona fide troublemaker and if you have anything to do with him, he'll ruin your life.

Leave him alone. Stay away from anything that even closely resembles him or his temptations. He has some mighty neat schemes up his sleeve to lure you away from your Heavenly Father, so don't be deceived. Believe James 4:7b which promises, *...Resist the devil and he will flee from you.* Then exercise the authority you have through Jesus Christ and say, *...Get thee behind me, Satan...* (Luke 4:8).

God, on the other hand, has some grand things in store for you, and you don't have to wait until you get to Heaven to receive them. One of them is the *peace* in knowing that after you die you will spend your eternity with Christ in Heaven. You and I received this *peace* when we first believed in Jesus Christ. *For God so loved the world, that He gave His only begotten Son, that <u>whosoever believeth in Him should not perish, but have everlasting life</u>* (John 3:16, emphasis added).

Romans 10:9 promised us and now promises other lost people, *That if thou shalt confess with thy mouth the Lord Jesus, and shalt believe in thine heart that God hath raised Him from the dead, thou shalt be saved.* That's all there is to it!

When you and I accepted Jesus as our Lord and Savior, Satan was notified immediately that he had lost our souls and now had two more enemies to contend with. At that moment, he became concerned that you and I might just be two of those "shonuf" Believers who would amount to something for Jesus. Who knows, you and I may be the ones whom God has chosen to cause significant havoc in the realm of hell and disrupt Satan's plans to corrupt the whole of mankind.

As Mike Shirley, a fellow Hellfighter, puts it, "The thing that scares the devil to death is seeing his former servants with Bibles in their hands leading men to Jesus!"

History records that every now and then, a Believer comes along who excels above the rest, men like: Moses, Elijah, Jeremiah, David, Martin Luther, William Tyndale, Billy Graham, Gray Allison, Jerry Falwell, Harold Danley, Bailey Smith, Adrian Rogers, Bob Kendrick and, of course, Paige Patterson. It will take great courage and tenacity to join their ranks and take your place beside the likes of them on the frontlines of the battle. But you can and will, IF you've got what it takes!

You see, Satan has dealt these old boys misery over the years, and has probably dealt you some too. But they have prevailed against his onslaught. **Have you?** They have won their battles against Satan because they all mastered something that every Hellfighter must master.

What did they master? They mastered the Bible, that's what. The precious Word of God; His Guidebook for victorious living; His Rule Book for our lives. It is every Christian's source for *defense*. To Hellfighters, however, it is the greatest source for *offensive* tactics that we have against our most dangerous adversary, Satan. The Bible teaches us not only to defend our faith, but also to exercise our faith by attacking the enemy's strongholds. Ephesians 6:12 tells us, *For we wrestle not against flesh and blood, but against principalities, against powers, against the rulers of the darkness of this world, against spiritual wickedness in high places.*

The Bible is a gift from God, just like your salvation. Even though you may have purchased your Bible or were given one by a friend, it is still a gift from the Giver of your eternal security.

This gift that God prepared for us years ago is the only tool we have that is capable of forging our individual Weapons of Faith from tiny little Pocketknives into impressive battle Swords. Nothing can take the place of the Bible in this regard. His Holy Word is the ultimate provider of our strength and courage, and it is essential that you master its contents, if you desire to live the Christ-like life as a Hellfighter.

2 Timothy 3:16, 17 (NKJV) tells us that *All Scripture is given by inspiration of God, and is profitable for doctrine, for reproof, for correction, for instruction in righteousness, that the man of God may be complete, thoroughly equipped for every good work.*

When you received your first Bible, it was probably untried and unproven by you. I hope you've worked hard to master it. **Have you?** I hope you've disciplined yourself to learn its mysteries, its strengths and its characteristics, and that you're letting it teach you how to unleash the power that's within you. Either you will allow God's Biblical promises to motivate you to be a valiant warrior (a.k.a. Hellfighter) for Christ or you will reject those promises, spurn His wisdom and consequently fail life's test.

As you master the Bible's secrets, and gain deeper knowledge from its truths, your faith will grow by leaps and bounds. Soon you will become more and more dependent upon God's Word, not only for your survival against Satan's temptations, but also to win great victories against him. The Bible is your only reliable source for an endless supply of the provisions necessary for the battles ahead. Everything you need for any situation can be found there.

The combination of Biblical knowledge and a Believer's faith in Jesus Christ form our most decisive weapons in our fight against Satan. These Weapons of Faith are given to those of us who really believe that Jesus is the King of kings and Lord of lords.

As you read earlier, your faith in Jesus Christ may still be small, insignificant, and maybe even weak, just like a pocketknife. So, let's take a minute to examine your faith and find out how big and strong it actually is.

Is your faith a formidable weapon or is it still so miniscule that its size is immeasurable? In other words, does the faith you have in Jesus and the knowledge you have of the Word of God measure up? Is your faith still the size of a pocketknife or is it now the size of a sword? If it's only the size of a pocketknife, it means you're only scratching the surface of God's secrets. This means you need to get busy and start studying God's Word like you should! Faith, like an unused pocketknife, will become rusty and useless if you don't exercise it. Don't let that happen.

Your courage to do battle with the enemy was also weak when you first became a Christian. But, as you study the promises of your Bible and learn the mysteries within it, your confidence will grow and your courage will increase.

When studied and utilized daily, the Bible will provide the protection, security, strength and power necessary to be victorious over the enemy. When mastered, the Bible will show you how to storm the gates of hell and defeat that old serpent. In Matthew 16:18b, Jesus said, ...*I will build My church; and the gates of hell shall not prevail against it.* That means there's no stopping you!

As your faith in God and His Son Jesus grows, His revelation of Biblical truths along with His rules of engagement will become clear and meaningful to you. Once these magnificent weapons of conquest are sealed in your heart, then you can become the valiant warrior for Christ that He wants you to be.

> **C'mon man. Christ died for you. The least you can do is live for Him!**

As you continue to study diligently the truths and commands given to us in the Bible, you will surpass your wildest dreams of serving Him...

- *IF*...you've met Jesus face to face;
- *IF*...you're willing to pay the price to master your Bible;
- *IF*...you're willing to become an army of one;
- *IF*...you're willing to pledge your total allegiance to the Giver of your faith and...
- *IF*...you're willing to place complete confidence and trust in God's Word.

Then, and only then, will you have the distinct privilege of serving Jesus Christ as a Hellfighter.

LIFE IS A TEST.
IF YOU FAIL, IT'S HELL!

WHATSOEVER THY HAND FINDETH TO DO, DO IT WITH [ALL] THY MIGHT…

ECCLESIASTES 9:10A

CHAPTER 3

The Pocketknife of Immature Faith

Are you a new Christian whose faith is only the size of a pocketknife? As you learn more about God's Word, your Pocketknife-sized Faith will grow and you'll be surprised at the power available to you. The more you read your Bible and the more you study its tactics, the more you will discover that its strategy to defeat the enemy is very sound. Very soon, if you keep studying, your Weapon of Faith will no longer be compared to the size of a pocketknife but to the size of a two-handed, battle sword.

Isn't it exciting to know that the power and capability of your Weapon of Faith will grow as your knowledge of the Bible and His power swell within you? It's a good thing too, because you can't be on the frontlines of the battle with faith that compares to the size of a pocketknife, now can you?

Maybe, you're not a new Christian! Maybe you've been a Believer for a long time but your faith still compares to the size of a pocketknife. If this is the case, you must do something about it! Don't you think?

> **The amount of time it takes for your Weapon of Faith to achieve its maximum potential is dependent upon how much love you have for Jesus.**

If you have been a Christian for sometime now and your faith and knowledge of God's Word still remain small, you may want to ask yourself what you've been doing all this time. You must not have been studying your Bible and talking to God like you should've. My goodness, man, your Pocketknife-sized Faith should be comparable to a sword by now! As a matter of fact, your Pocketknife-sized Faith should have begun increasing in size the moment you were saved.

Let's pretend, for instance, that it's Sunday morning, you scrubbed the dirt off last night, your deodorant is working, your cologne is smelling good, your clothes are clean, your hair is combed, but...oops, you did it again! You got to church and you forgot your Bible. Doggone it, you didn't mean to leave it on your dresser, where it doubles as a dust catcher, did you? I guess it was covered up with something. No, wait! Maybe it's still being used as your car's dashboard ornament since the last time you went to church. Oh my, haven't you even read it since then?

I hope this is not you, but if it is, it means your faith is still only the size of a puny, little pocketknife.

Maybe you're satisfied with Pocketknife-sized Faith! Maybe you're one of those Christians who likes to keep your faith concealed so that it's not conspicuous and no one will even know you have it until you decide to show it, **like when you're at church!** If this describes you, there are two verses of Scripture you need to think about, *Whosoever therefore shall confess Me before men, him will I confess also before My Father which is in Heaven. But whosoever shall deny Me before men, him will I also deny before My Father which is in Heaven* (Matthew 10:32, 33).

However, if you're not satisfied having only Pocketknife-sized Faith, let me ask you some questions so we can find out why your faith is not growing like it should.

How's your church attendance? Do you attend church regularly or do you feel that "corporate worship" is unnecessary? Maybe if you recognized the importance of it, your faith and knowledge of God's Word would compare to something more than just a mere pocketknife. God knew we would second-guess the whole church thing. That's why He warned us about it in Hebrews 10:25 when He told us not to forsake the assembling of ourselves together!

What about your prayer life? Is it dull and unfulfilling? Do you have to tell God who you are each time you pray? Does so much time pass between prayers that God no longer recognizes your voice? Maybe this is why your prayers go unanswered.

God does *hear* the prayers of men with Pocketknife-sized Faith, but he *answers* the prayers of those who exercise their faith like true champions.

Does a bedtime "prayerette" suffice for a good feeling before you go to bed? In reality, a "prayerette" is like waving at a stranger whom you'll never have the privilege of knowing intimately. Men with Sword-sized faith say prayers, not prayerettes.

What about sharing the Gospel with others? It's hard to tell someone about something you know very little about, isn't it? If somebody were to ask you about Jesus, what would you tell 'em? Would you have all the right answers? Could you locate the Scriptures necessary to lead that person to Christ? Now, there's a question to ponder, huh!

If you think that was a good question, then sink your teeth into this one. *If you were arrested for being a Christian, would there be enough evidence to convict you?* Considering the size of your Weapon

What good is it to be a Christian if you don't intend to exercise your faith?

of Faith, what would a jury say about you?

2 Timothy 2:15 says, *Study to shew thyself approved unto God, a workman that needeth not to be ashamed, rightly dividing the Word of Truth.* You'll never have abundant faith until you study your Bible diligently.

LIFE IS A TEST.
IF YOU FAIL, IT'S HELL!

...But when they have heard, Satan cometh immediately, and taketh away the Word that was sown in their hearts.

Mark 4:15b

CHAPTER 4

The Cutlass of Maturing Faith

re you a good example of what a Christian is supposed to be and do? Do you reflect Christ with your smile? Do you radiate Christ with every word you speak and deed you do? Do you go to church as often as you should? Do you study God's Word as often as you should? Do you tell others about Jesus like you know you should? Is the cover of your Bible a little worn around the edges?

If you can answer "Yes" to these questions, then you're making progress and your faith is maturing. The reality of what loving Jesus is all about is beginning to show through these new traits that you now possess. These traits prove that a little study and a little knowledge of the Word of God will accomplish much in your walk with Christ.

Have you ever thought about what would really happen if you studied the Bible as you should? If not, let me tell you what will happen. Amazing things, my brother, AMAZING THINGS! Listen to what the prophet Jeremiah recorded in God's Word, *Call unto Me, and I will answer thee, and shew thee great and mighty things, which thou knowest not* (Jeremiah 33:3). By applying yourself, your Pocketknife-sized Faith will grow into Cutlass-sized Faith.

Do you not only attend church on Sunday morning, but also go back to church on Sunday night? If you do, that's great! But, do you listen to what the preacher is saying or are you preoccupied with what you'll do when church is over? If you go to church just to go to church, you're wasting your time. Remember, going to church doesn't make you a Hellfighter any more than going to McDonald's makes you a hamburger. Regular church attendance is very important, not only because fellowship with other Believers is necessary, but also because it is an outward expression of your love for Jesus and a good example for others to follow. God isn't the only one who watches your actions; those around you also watch every move you make. Satan, too, is taking notice. He's watching to see whether or not he needs to be fearful of you.

I have a pastor friend who leads a church of over 700 members. Three to four hundred are in regular attendance each Sunday, but my pastor friend says there's only one man in his church who he can count on to be there every time the doors open. My friend says this faithful servant, whose name is Larry, is the only "constant" he has in his church. In other words, Satan only has to be concerned about one man, besides the pastor, in this church of 700.

If this was your church, and you weren't the pastor, would you be that one man? *Are you* one of the few Hellfighters in your church or are you just a pew-warming, Sunday morning Christian? Consistency and faithfulness are signs of maturing faith.

Are you attending the various programs offered by your church? If so, you're building relationships with fellow Believers and that's very important. Christian friends will hold you accountable and help you do what is right.

Are you participating in overseas mission projects? *Are you* ministering locally to those less fortunate than you? *Are you* finding it easier to tell others about Jesus? Remember what James 1:22a says, *be ye doers of the Word, and not hearers only…*

Your faith will never get any stronger than it is right now unless you step up your training and master the mysteries of your Bible. It will require extreme dedication and unreserved discipline to master its contents. But, if you'll pay the price to do it, you will become a valiant Hellfighter for Jesus. Obedience is another sign of maturing faith.

Think about this next question! *Are you* one of those Hellfighter-wannabes who knows just enough about the Word of God to look, act and talk spiritual? If so, remember this, it's easy to fool those who know very little about the Word of God! But we don't want to go around fooling people, now do we? Genuineness is a sure sign of maturing faith. Genuine Hellfighters are properly trained and adequately prepared servants of the most high God. *Are you?*

Your Bible, even though your knowledge of it may be marginal, has unlimited resources. The maturity of your faith, however, is the key to unlocking its wealth of ultimate power and unbounded authority.

Like I said earlier, you may think you're a Hellfighter, but if you're not studying God's Word like you should, then you aren't!

The strength of your faith is also dependent upon the level of conversation you have each day with your Heavenly Father. Are your prayers one way conversations in which you tell Him what you want, need and expect, say "amen," and off you go? If so, this ain't praying! This is requestin' and it means that your Cutlass-sized Faith has some more maturing to do.

My Bible says in James 5:16b, and so does yours, that, *The effectual fervent prayer of a righteous man availeth much.* Are you a righteous person? Are your prayers being heard? Are you prayin' or just requestin'?

How's your daily walk with Christ? Are you living the Christ-like life; or do some *sins* still have control over you? Do you still participate in a little partying here and there? Do you still partake of a sip or two of the brew, a little snort of coke or a suck on a joint? Or is your personal sin a quick peek or two at the web chicks?

Don't go getting ticked off at me now; I know what you're thinking. Yeah, you're thinking that these are personal *sins* and they're no big deal; you're thinking that *sins* like these only affect *you*, right? Wrong! *Your sins* affect the entire Kingdom of God. If you're not pure, holy and righteous, then you're compromising your personal testimony and you're falling right into Satan's web of deceit.

But maybe you think you're smarter than that, huh? Maybe you think you can outfox the devil! If you do, then there's something you need to know and you need to know it right now...*you will never outfox Satan, he'll outfox you* because he's smarter than you are and much more experienced. As a matter of fact, he's working overtime to ruin your life and this is how he'll do it:

- He'll suck the *happiness* out of your life with drugs!
- He'll suck the *reliability* out of your commitments with alcohol!
- He'll suck the *romance* out of a happy relationship through premarital or extramarital sex!
- He'll suck the *joy* out of your life by destroying your relationship with Christ!
- He'll suck the *peace* out of your life by persuading you to compromise your convictions!
- He'll suck the *quality* out of your character and turn you into a sniveling weasel!
- He'll suck the *integrity* out of your reputation!
- He'll suck the *fun* out of your relationship with your kids!
- He'll suck the *will* to resist him out of you if you keep dabbling in his arena of pleasures!

In other words, SATAN SUCKS and don't forget it!

Consider this: Have you made a lot of progress in your walk with Christ and in your knowledge of His Word? Has your Weapon of Faith increased from Pocketknife-size to Cutlass-size? If so, beware! All can be lost with one act of foolish disobedience.

> The influence of your Weapon of Faith is minor if you don't utilize its authority and master its power.

Does the exercising of your faith indicate to you that you're doing most things right? If so, continue to be faithful and master the power of your faith, which God freely gives to those who faithfully follow Him. Then you can move to the next level of service. But, beware! It could be most dangerous!

1 Peter 5:8 tells us to, *Be sober, be vigilant; because your adversary the devil, as a roaring lion, walketh about, seeking whom he may devour.* The "whom" in this passage is YOU!

It appears that most Christians get to a point in their walk with Christ where they're comfortable and complacent. They think they have reached the pinnacle of their service to God when in reality, most Christians remain as immature as babies; as a matter of fact, some never mature.

Until you decide you're not satisfied with Pocketknife-sized or Cutlass-sized Faith and make your mind up to mature even more in your walk with Christ, you could be a "downfall" waiting to happen. If you're not willing or just don't have the courage to take the next step, be warned. You will either remain behind the camouflage of mediocrity that has kept you out of Satan's line of site or you will step out of your comfort zone and suit up for battle.

You may think he's dealt you misery up to this point, but if your faith is just Pocketknife-sized or Cutlass-sized, you haven't been worth Satan' trouble. From this point on it's a whole different ballgame for you. If you bow up and mean business, you'll no longer be wielding just a Cutlass! You'll be wielding a Jeweled Sword of Obedient Faith.

NOW THEREFORE,
IF YE WILL OBEY
MY VOICE,
AND KEEP MY
COVENANT,
THEN YE SHALL
BE A PECULIAR
TREASURE UNTO
ME ABOVE ALL
PEOPLE...

EXODUS 19:5A

CHAPTER 5

The Jeweled Sword of Obedient Faith

 od says in Jeremiah 33:3, *Call unto Me, and I will answer thee, and shew thee great and mighty things, which thou knowest not.*

With the kind of knowledge God wants to give you, you should feel very important. Some folks, when given the opportunity to gain such knowledge, let it go to their head. They become cocky and conceited; kind of like a know-it-all. Don't let this happen to you. Always remain humble like Jesus.

Think about this! Are you going to church because you want to, not because you feel that you have to? Are you attending Sunday morning services, Sunday evening services, and Wednesday night services? Are you going to visitation or participating in community outreach ministries? Is your whole week centered around the things of God? If so, your obedience pleases our Heavenly Father and your maturing process is well underway. This means that your faith is standing out. It's shining like a Jeweled Sword!

Do you enjoy reading your Bible? Or more importantly, do you enjoy *studying* it? Are new truths being revealed to you that were not revealed to you the last time you read certain passages? Is your study of God's Word unlocking more power for your faith? Can you feel God's power in His promises? Is your faithfulness to the Author of your faith more steadfast now than it's ever been? If so, it means that your Weapon of Faith has grown in size from a Cutlass into a beautifully

Jeweled Sword of Obedient Faith. And, Satan is taking notice.

Is the frequency with which you use your Weapon of Faith increasing every day? Is the skill with which you exercise your faith more tenacious and bold? If so, I'm sure that Jesus is well pleased with you!

Is your prayer life doing pretty good? Is your goodnight prayer no longer just a casual goodnight "prayerette," but a grateful prayer of thanksgiving for a glorious and productive day? Do you pray before you leave to go to work or school each day? Are you saying "hello" to Jesus several times a day? Do you feel His presence throughout the day? Actually, I would hope that you are now on a first name basis with God and that He no longer has to ask your name when you call upon Him!

My sheep hear My voice, and I know them, and they follow Me (John 10:27).

Are you exercising your faith by telling others about Jesus? Do you excitedly tell others about the gift of His Salvation, which He's so freely given to you? Do you open the Word of God regularly, and share its wonderful truths with those who are lost? Does your knowledge of God's Word allow you to reveal the truths of the Gospel stories? Are you now helping others realize how truly special they are to Jesus? That's how someone with a Jeweled Sword of Obedient Faith serves God.

Do you go so far as to tell everyone you meet that they too will be favored with their free gift from the Giver if they will only accept Him as their Lord and Savior? Matthew 7:7 gives us a wonderful promise, *Ask, and it shall be given you; seek, and ye shall find; knock, and it shall be opened unto you.*

Are your faith and courage growing? Do you feel as if you're really making progress? Are you leading people to Christ? If so...Satan is about to take you on! He can't stand men who have gained a wealth of godly knowledge and spiritual enthusiasm. Your success could cause your faith to be tested. You're now right where Satan wants you to be...because he likes flashy Christians! Those are the ones he likes to tear down!

Where you are now, in your walk with Christ, is kind of like flying an airplane for the first time; you've learned just enough to get yourself into trouble!

There's an old saying that goes something like this, "There's always calm before the storm." This calm indicates that trouble is brewing! You can't see it coming, you can't feel it coming, you can't hear it coming, but very soon the demons of hell may come knocking on your front door. They may be knocking now.

> **For if a man think himself to be something when he is nothing, he deceiveth himself.**
>
> GALATIANS 6:3

> **When pride cometh, then cometh shame...**
>
> PROVERBS 11:2A

> **In his self-sufficiency he will be in distress; Every hand of misery will come against him.**
>
> JOB 20:22 (NKJV)

When you start serving God as you should and the calm, peaceful presence of Christ fills your life, that's when Satan unleashes his fury. That's why you must wield, with equal fury, God's Jeweled Sword of Obedient Faith and utilize all the armor that goes with it. So, do as Ephesians 6:11 says, *Put on the whole armour of God, that ye may be able to stand against the wiles of the devil.*

Before you become a victim of Satan's onslaught— get prepared!

- Don't wait until Satan attacks to start studying God's Word! Study it NOW!
- Don't wait to ask God for courage! Ask for it NOW!
- Don't wait to put on the whole armor of God! Put it on NOW!
- Don't be deceived into thinking that you're strong enough to fight Satan unprepared! Increase your faith in God NOW!

Satan will pounce on you from out of nowhere. He will attack when you least expect it! He's searching for your weaknesses and that's where he'll strike. So put up a towering wall of defense by **memorizing strategic Scriptures!** They will increase your ability to defend yourself. But remember, when you're dueling with the enemy, don't be deceived into thinking that just because you've earned the privilege to wield a Jeweled Sword that you're invincible. Don't be lulled into believing the propaganda that says, "Satan doesn't even know you exist." Believe me, brother, if you're a Hellfighter, he has a MOST WANTED poster, with your mug shot on it, hanging on the charred walls of hell's post office!

The more knowledgeable you are about God's Word the more effective you'll be as a Hellfighter! But beware, the more effective you are for Christ, the more attention Satan will pay to your strengths and weaknesses. In other words, the stronger your faith gets, the madder Satan gets!

Don't think you'll escape his onslaught. It will come, and it will come when it is most opportune for him and least expected by you. Be ready! Be prepared! Be vigilant! Be obedient and obtain, through greater dedication and uncompromising faith, the Christian's Sword of Defensive Faith. Then give that old devil a dose of where he lives.

LIFE IS A TEST.
IF YOU FAIL, IT'S HELL!

DO NOT BE AFRAID OF SUDDEN TERROR, NOR OF TROUBLE FROM THE WICKED WHEN IT COMES.

PROVERBS 3:25 (NKJV)

CHAPTER 6

The Christian's Sword of Defensive Faith

n the movie *The Three Musketeers*, it was "all for one and one for all." Each musketeer had individual skirmishes, but when the chips were down they all rallied together and with their three swords steeled together in unison, they always defeated their foe.

We, too, have a Trinity upon which you and I can certainly rely for everything. Our Trinity is the Father, the Son and the Holy Spirit. These three are also known as the Creator, the Giver and the Motivator.

GOD, the Father, *created* everything for our enjoyment. JESUS, the Son, is the *Giver* of eternal life and the provider of our faith, from which we draw our power. The HOLY SPIRIT is the One who *motivates* Believers into action.

In this chapter, you'll find out if your success and dedication to Jesus have gotten you into trouble with Satan himself; if so, you'll quickly realize that only a proven Hellfighter can be victorious. Your loyalty and obedience to our Lord Jesus Christ has, up to this point, been represented by your Jeweled Sword of Obedient Faith. It is now, however, necessary for your weapon to be increased. Your maturity and total commitment to Jesus Christ is now represented by The Christian's Sword of Defensive Faith.

Your faith and walk with the Lord must now be strong and mighty. You must be as unafraid and as valiant as the Three Musketeers were when they defended their king's realm from the aggression of their enemies. A Hellfighter must always be prepared to defend himself and his stand for Jesus Christ.

God's Word commands us in Proverbs 3:5 to, *Trust in the LORD with all thine heart; and lean not unto thine own understanding.* If you exercise obedience and faithfulness to Him, He will sustain you regardless of what Satan hurls at you. Joshua 1:9 (NKJV) gives us these words of encouragement, *"... Be strong and of good courage; do not be afraid, nor be dismayed, for the LORD your God is with you wherever you go."*

You're moving into the league with the big boys now, Hellfighter! So, I hope you know how to utilize your Weapon of Faith. I hope you've learned enough about God's Word to unleash its power and thus defend yourself against Satan's assault! You must be prepared; you must spend endless hours memorizing the promises

> **Remember to clothe yourself in the whole armor of God. You can do that by learning everything there is to know about God's Word.**

of God's Word. Unless you dedicate yourself to the study of God's Word and learn its secrets and master its truths, your defenses may still be breached.

Ephesians 6:11a tells us to *Put on the whole armour of God...* Is your helmet on? Is your breastplate in place? Is your sword in your hand? Is God's wisdom in your heart? If so, you should be ready to defend your faith! But, where is Satan? Where is the enemy? Where are his forces?

Did you think he was going to be blatant about his assault? No way, José! Satan is subtle and sly like a fox. 2 Corinthians 11:14 warns us that, ... *Satan himself is transformed into an angel of light,* even though he is actually the Prince of Darkness.

Remember, he's a deceiver so he'll try to weaken your stand for Christ through simple temptations at first. And, if you ever start to show a little complacency here, or a little negligence there... BAM! Before you know it, you'll be defeated and your testimony for Christ will be in shambles.

Satan and his band of seducing, demonic, warriors will slip up on you, brother! And believe me they'll do whatever it takes to ruin you! Just look at the following examples to see if I'm telling the truth:

TOBACCO – This will probably be the first bullet he fires at you. After all, it's not that bad; smoking just stinks and causes cancer, that's all.

Remember, Satan hates your guts and he would love to attack your body, the temple of God, with the big "C"…Cancer. The word cigarette also begins with the letter "C." Both are detrimental to your health, so why not stay away from cigarettes? If you do, chances are you'll stay clear of the big "C."

BEER – Umm! It's the gusto of life! Isn't it? At least that's what the TV commercials used to say. But, I bet the commercials lied!

I know some "good ole boys" who can drink a case of beer at a time, never get drunk and never give any thought to it being wrong. But, when you've got a gut as big as a washtub from drinking it by the case, I guess not.

If you're a beer drinker and you call yourself a Christian, you should be ashamed. Beer, whether it's bad for your health or not, is many times the introduction to far more harmful and addictive things. Beer is also associated with the honky-tonk, party-hardy lifestyle. That kind of lifestyle doesn't reflect Christ. The Bible says in 1 Thessalonians 5:22, *Abstain from all appearance of evil.* You can't do that while "popping a top."

ALCOHOL – Now this is another story. It will definitely mess you up!

> You may say you believe that alcohol will never possess your life. But, if you're a drinker, why can't you stop?

Satan would like for you to believe his lies: "Alcohol isn't addictive. It won't hurt *you*, you're invincible!"

I've had many friends wind up on the wrong side of the tracks, alone and distraught because of alcohol. They died broke and in the gutter because of this poison. Their last words were, "I never thought this would happen to me; I never thought this would happen to me!" IS IT HAPPENING TO YOU?

PORNOGRAPHY – This is the hottest thing outta the pits of hell! Nudity has been with us since time began. Today, however, nudity, and the flaunting of it as merchandise, is being marketed around the world as casually as Coca-Cola. You can't even open a magazine or turn on the TV anymore without being exposed to some form of lewdness. In advertisements, sensuality is being used to sell virtually everything from clothing to bathroom tissue.

> *"The only sure way for you not to become an alcoholic is to never let the first drop touch your lips."*
>
> ~ A.B. HEADRICK (MY DAD)

Satan will try to convince you that pornography isn't bad! He'll try to justify it by saying things like, "God Himself looked at Eve in the garden; if it's good enough for Him, it's good enough for you!" He'll continue by saying, "Some people claim that pornography creates hideous desires and brings out secret lusts that can only be satisfied by rape, incest, child abuse and even brutality. That's not true—it's all in their minds!" Yes, that's what he wants you to believe, but remember, Satan is a liar!

Statistics say 9 out of 10 Children between the ages of 8 and 16 have viewed pornography in some form on the Internet. In most cases, the sex sites were accessed unintentionally when a child, often in the process of doing homework, used a seemingly innocent sounding word to search for information or pictures.

Reports show that over 40 million Americans visit cyber-sex sites regularly. In a recent poll, fifty-one percent of pastors admitted that cyber porn is a possible temptation; the other forty-nine percent need to wake up!

Currently, there are over 70 million pornographic search engine requests daily and over 400 million pages of pornography on the web readily available for viewing. And these numbers are increasing daily. It's astounding to say the least!

However, Satan would have you believe his $100 billion per year worldwide industry is nothing to be alarmed about. His producers of this mind-altering garbage say, "It's not habit forming." What do *you* believe?

Ahh, not habit forming, huh? Then it won't hurt if you take a peek, right? Wrong! Talk to anyone who's been seduced into Internet pornography and they'll tell you how one little peek can not only hurt you, but also pervert you and cripple your walk with the Lord. *But each one is tempted when he is carried away and enticed by his own lust. Then when lust has conceived, it gives birth to sin; and when sin is accomplished, it brings forth death* (James 1:14, 15, NASB).

DRUGS – This is where the demons of hell want you to believe true freedom is! Be smart and don't listen when they say to you, "Drugs won't burn your brain out! OK, OK, so a few of your friends OD'd, there are exceptions to everything, no big deal. Go ahead, try it!"

It may seem cool to try marijuana, but experimentation can quickly escalate to addiction. If you let Satan get a hook in you, he won't let go without a long, grueling fight. Most drug addicts say when they started smoking pot they had no intentions of becoming an addict. Marijuana opens the door to harder drugs like cocaine and meth, which seem like fun for the moment, however, before you realize it, you'll become their slave.

Read these horrifying words written by someone who has been there:

I'll destroy your home, and tear your family apart.
I'll steal your children, and that's just a start.
I'm more valued than diamonds, more precious than gold.
The sorrow I bring, is a sight to behold.

If you need me, remember, I'm easily found.
I live all around you, in schools and in town.
I live with the rich, I live with the poor,
I live down the street, maybe next door.

I'm made in a lab, but not one like you think.
I'm sometimes made under your sink.
I'm made in your closets, and in the woods.
If this scares you to death, it certainly should.

I have many names, but there's one you know best.
I'm sure you've heard of me, my name's Crystal Meth.
My power is awesome, just try me and see.
But if you do, you may never break free.

Try me just once, and I might let you go,
but try me twice, and I'll own your soul.

When I possess you, you'll steal and you'll lie.
You'll do whatever it takes to get high.

The crimes you'll commit for my narcotic charms,
will be worth the pleasure you'll feel in my arms.
You'll lie to your mother, and steal from your dad.
When you see their tears, you'll never feel sad.

You'll forget your morals and how you were raised.
Then I'll be your conscience, and teach you my ways.
I take kids from their parents, and parents from their kids.
I turn people from God, and I separate friends.

I'll take everything from you, your looks and your pride.
I'll be with you always, right by your side.
You'll give up everything, family and home,
your money and friends, then you'll be alone.

I'll take and take, till you've no more to give,
including your purpose and will to live.
If you try me be warned, this is not a game.
If given the chance, I'll drive you insane.

I'll ravage your body, and control your mind.
I'll own you completely, your soul will be mine.
I'll give you a nightmare when you're in your bed.
And voices you'll hear, from inside your head.

The sweats and shakes, and the visions you'll see,
I want you to know, they're all gifts from me.
But then it's too late, and you'll know in your heart,
that you are now mine, and we shall never part.

You'll regret that you tried me (they always do).
But you came to me, not me to you.
You never thought this would happen, though you were told.
But you challenged my powers, and chose to be bold.

You should have said no, and then walked away.
If you could live that day over, now what would you say?
My powers are awesome, as I told you before.
I'll take your life, and make it hunger for more.

I'll be your master, and you'll be my slave.
And then I'll take you straight to your grave.
Now that you've met me, what will you do?
Will you give me a try? It's all up to you.

I can show you more misery than words can tell.
Come, take my hand, and I'll lead you to hell!!!
So now that you know me, what will YOU do?
Take MY advice and DON'T BE A FOOL!

Author Unknown

Satan wants you to believe that drug abuse is America's culture; that it's today's happening thing. But, it isn't America's culture. It's Satan's deception! Don't buy into it – not even once!

America's cultural heritage is the land of the free and the home of the brave. Mainstream media, however, wants every American to believe we've become a sub-culture of drunks, crack-heads and perverts, but we haven't. Check the viewings of *The Passion of the Christ*. Overnight, it became one of the highest income-producing films of all time! Why? Because Christian Americans finally had something decent to go see. We are many in number but the weapons of our faith are weak and rusty. Their jewels have lost their sparkle and the fire that tempered our blades is cold because of our unfaithfulness to the Giver, Jesus Christ.

SEX – Yep, this is the big one! I don't have to explain the birds and the bees to you, you know very well how it works. Sex is a wonderful gift from God, but it is intended only for marriage. Abstinence before marriage pleases God; fornication before marriage displeases Him. Faithful partners are a blessing to Him, but adultery after marriage makes God want to puke.

Deuteronomy 11:26-28a warns us, *Behold, I set before you this day a blessing and a curse; A blessing, if ye obey the commandments of the LORD your God, which I command you this day: And a curse, if ye will not obey the commandments of the LORD your God...* My daddy used to paraphrase this passage for me like this "obedience brings blessings; disobedience brings a curse."

If you're an unmarried person, WAIT! Yes, wait for marriage to have sex with the love of your life. Your wedding night will be a special night for both of you, if you wait! If you don't wait, and your bride is not your "first," why should she ever believe she will be your last? Waiting will bring great blessings!

In Proverbs chapter 7, the Bible tells us to seek wisdom and understanding so that we will not get caught in Satan's web of deceit. Verses 17 and 18 of that same chapter give us an example of how a man who lacks wisdom could very easily be seduced by a woman controlled by Satan. Her words are coaxing and convincing; *I have perfumed my bed with myrrh, aloes, and cinnamon. Come, let us take our fill of love until morning; Let us delight ourselves with love* (NKJV).

Don't fall prey to the temptations of Satan's seducing spirits. Remember, he hates your guts and has no intentions of doing anything good for you. **Satan wants you to believe his lies:** "Sex is OK! Everybody's doing it! This stuff about syphilis, gonorrhea, AIDS and V.D., that's just a bunch of hype. It's coming from old folks who are jealous because they're afraid you'll have more fun than they did!"

Satan is a deceiver who wants you to live in his world of double-speak. He wants you to believe that good is bad and bad is good. He wants you to believe that right is wrong and wrong is right. WHAT DO YOU BELIEVE?

Oh, but he's got more ways to skin your hide than tobacco, beer, alcohol, pornography, drugs and sex. There's the love of money, materialism, power, envy, jealousy, deceit and bitterness…just to name a few.

So, keep your sword drawn, Hellfighter! When anything that is foreign to the teachings of God raises its ugly head, use your Sword of Defensive Faith to rid yourself of its temptations. James 4:7b encourages us to, *Resist the devil and he will flee from you.*

How do you feel you're progressing? Is the battle between you and Satan going your way? Are you passing the test of combat with flying colors? Is your heart and soul clean and pure? Are you refraining from participating in Satan's carousel of temptations? If so, this means your faith is growing. The power of God that is within you is fortifying you against Satan's attacks. To be victorious, however, it is imperative that God be in total control of your life!

Let's take a little test and see how you score when answering these questions:

- If every Christian was as prepared for battle as YOU are, what kind of army would we have?
- If every Christian read their Bible as often as YOU do, how much knowledge would we have to share with the lost?

- If every Christian bent their knees in prayer as often as YOU do, what kind of prayer warriors would we be?
- If every Christian shared the Gospel as often as YOU do, how many would hear about Jesus today?
- If every Christian was just like YOU, what kind of Christian would every Christian be?

Hurts doesn't it? Yes, it does! I reeled myself when I wrote that.

You see, Satan mobilized against you long before your weapon became the size and strength of a Christian's Sword of Defensive Faith. But, thanks be to Jesus, you've been able to overcome Satan's temptations of the past or you wouldn't be where you are today. Just remember this, Satan has an endless amount of tenacity and he won't stop trying to discredit and/or destroy you until you're dead! Right this minute he's on the move to ruin your life and to destroy your testimony.

If you're being true to God's Word, you've really ticked Satan off! If he's not winning the battle against you, believe me, brother, he won't give up!

Even though he knows he's already lost your soul and that his attempts to discredit you have failed up to now, he will not back down.

Yes, Satan may concede some battles to you, but if he does, watch out! It may be a ploy to make you think the heat is off. Don't be fooled; he will eventually bring his whole arsenal into play against you.

If you've been coasting for a while and there're no spiritual battles raging in your life right now, it could be that his subtle approach is about to be over. Maybe he's getting ready to launch a full-scale attack against you. But if you remain steadfast and faithful to the Giver of the power within your Bible, and have His treasures hidden deep within your heart, you'll be OK. Be sure, however, that all the treasures you cherish are kingdom focused, not worldly pleasures. The Bible tells us in Matthew 6:19, 20, *Lay not up for yourselves treasures upon earth, where moth and rust doth corrupt, and where thieves break through and steal: But lay up for yourselves treasures in Heaven, where neither moth nor rust doth corrupt, and where thieves do not break through nor steal.*

Proverbs 4:20-22 says, *My son, attend to My words; incline thine ear unto My sayings. Let them not depart from thine eyes; keep them in the midst of thine heart. For they are life unto those that find them, and health to all their flesh.*

Are you defeating Satan with your Sword of Defensive Faith? Have you shown Satan, by your dedication to God, that you're the real McCoy? Have you shown him that you didn't come this far to be defeated by some "has been" angel? Does Satan know that you are a Hellfighter and that there is now no turning back for you?

Hallelujah! You're resisting temptation from every side and you're not caving in. Your knowledge of God's Word has made you stronger spiritually than you've ever been and your exploits and victories are an encouragement to others. Your name is becoming synonymous with courage and character. Your faithfulness to our Heavenly Father is a blessing to all who know you. You are becoming a champion of the faith. You're becoming a David in a modern day world. You're the man! But…you had better be on the lookout; that old serpent, that old dragon, that old devil, who is Satan, still hates your guts. So, don't get complacent, my friend. Keep striving to develop a deeper degree of tenacity that will extend the reach of your Sword of Defensive Faith even further.

Sachel Paige, that great baseball player of the 20th century, said, "Never look back, 'cause something may be gaining on you." In your case, it could be Satan!

LIFE IS A TEST.
IF YOU FAIL, IT'S HELL!

YEA, THOUGH I
WALK THROUGH
THE VALLEY OF
THE SHADOW OF
DEATH, I WILL
FEAR NO EVIL: FOR
THOU ART WITH
ME; THY ROD AND
THY STAFF THEY
COMFORT ME.

PSALM 23:4

CHAPTER 7

The Hellfighter's Sword of Committed Faith

hen Sir William Wallace, aka BRAVEHEART, died in 1305, his last recorded word was "FREEDOM!" After that, his executioners ripped him open, pulled his guts out with their hands and beheaded him. Then they took his limbs and torso, hacked them to pieces and dispersed a piece of his body to all the provinces of Scotland. This act was a silent warning that no one else should lead a rebellion against Scottish authorities.

What does Sir William Wallace's death have to do with this book? A lot! Sir William Wallace was a freedom fighter and so are you. Sir William fought to free his countrymen from tyranny. You, Sir Christian, are called to free those who are bound by Satan's suppressive bonds of sin.

Sir William's sword was a mighty weapon. It took two hands to wield its powerful blade. Its weight and the force of its blow could easily behead his opponent.

You are achieving victory after victory by warding off Satan's attacks. In each battle, your Weapon of Faith has proven its strength and mighty power. Consequently, your faith can no longer be compared to a Pocketknife of Immature Faith, a Cutlass of Maturing Faith, a Jeweled Sword of Obedient Faith or to a Christian's Sword of Defensive Faith. Your Faith, as a weapon, has now become a mighty Sword of Committed Faith that can only be wielded by a Hellfighter for Christ.

Skirmishes with Satan will be a daily thing until you die, and you'll have to deal with each of them personally. But at some point in your life, there will come a time when you will have to let Satan know once and for all where you stand. It won't matter how young or how old you are when that time comes, Satan will still want to skin your hide! So you, too, must be thoroughly prepared to skin his!

As I said before, he realizes and concedes to the fact that he has lost your soul. But, he's still trying to figure out how to discredit you and to destroy your testimony for Christ. He knows you have a weak spot, and if he can just find it, you're dead meat!

You know you have a weak spot, too; that one little something that if Satan finds you in just the right place at just the right time he can have his way with you. You must never compromise your faith so that you find yourself in that position. One weak moment, one little "I can get by with it this time" attitude and everything you've worked so hard to achieve will be gone. Satan's whole purpose, as far as you're concerned, is to bring you down to his level and render you worthless to the Kingdom of God.

It may have taken you a lifetime to solidify your walk with Christ to such a degree that no one questions your faith. But, that doesn't matter to Satan, he'll still ruin you if he can.

There should now be enough evidence to prove that you're a true blue, 100%, til-death-do-you-serve-Jesus Hellfighter. Let's take a look and see how you stack up and if you're ready for Satan's next assault:

- Are you *studying* your Bible so much that its pages are tattered and torn?
- Are you *praying* so often that your carpet is threadbare, the knees of your britches are wearing thin and your knees are calloused?
- Are you a *faithful* and steadfast member of your local church?
- Are you a *tither*, giving 10% of your income to God?
- Are you a *giver*, giving over and above your 10% tithe?
- Are you *serving* in home and/or foreign missions by praying, giving and going?
- Are you *physically feeding* the hungry?
- Are you *giving* water to the thirsty?
- Are you *inviting* strangers to your church?

- Are you *clothing* those in need?
- Are you *visiting* the sick and those in prison?
- Are you *spiritually feeding* those who are hungry for God's Word with the Gospel message?
- Are you *telling* the spiritually thirsty about the Living Water that only Jesus has to offer?
- Are you *inviting* worldly sinners to come into the Kingdom of God through salvation?
- Are you *telling* those who are spiritually naked that their unrighteousness is as filthy rags, but Jesus can clothe them with garments white as snow?
- Are you *telling* those in sin that Jesus is the balm of Gilead and He can heal their sin-sick souls?
- And last, but not least, are you *giving* the prisoners of Satan's devilish enticements the keys that will unlock the chains of his demonic clutches?

If you have advanced to this arena of service for the King of kings, it means your faith can now be compared to a weapon as large as the Hellfighter's Sword of Committed Faith.

Very few Christians achieve this level of Christian responsibility. Hopefully you will remember the names of some of the men who fought in this same arena: David who killed Goliath; Daniel who survived the lion's den; Shadrach, Meshach and Abednego who survived the fiery furnace; Noah who overcame adversity, obeyed God and built the ark; Abraham who left his home and followed God; Moses who chose God over riches and led a nation to freedom; Joshua and Caleb who believed they could occupy the promised land and did; Peter who learned the hard way that serving Jesus is the "only way"; and Saul, the persecutor, who became Paul, the persecuted. This is the arena where only *real men* can compete. This is the battlefield that separates the men from the boys. This is frontline warfare and those with Pocketknife-sized Faith fail to qualify.

When you serve God in His league of extraordinary ladies and gentlemen, you are approaching legendary status. Hellfighters are those heroes of the faith who make things happen. They don't just sit around waiting for others to do something; they serve God while others watch!

Hellfighters engage the enemy while others talk about it in Sunday School!

Hellfighters are Christians who are no longer miserable when they go to church. Hellfighters long to worship their Lord Jesus Christ. Hellfighters long to pray, in fact, they consider it a privilege.

If the Bible has come alive to you and the hidden treasures within its pages are bursting forth as a fountain of living water within you, then you are a Hellfighter. Are you excited to be a Hellfighter? Are you motivated by the power of the Gospel? Are you constantly telling others about the Giver of your faith? If so, then you can consider yourself to be a faithful follower of Christ and a mighty warrior for the Kingdom of God – a Hellfighter! You are on your way toward becoming a true hero of the faith and, as such, you are even a greater threat to the Prince of Darkness.

Your service to the King of kings is not going unnoticed by Satan, and whether you like it or not you're on his radar screen! You are now one of hell's Most Wanted. And the legions of hell will soon be unleashed against you in full battle regalia. This time their attack will not be subtle; this time it will be ferocious; it could be disastrous if you're not prepared. Are you?

Get ready because here's what Satan openly desires to do to you: he wants to sacrifice you; he wants you to become a mockery to God; he wants you to fail at everything you put your hand to do!

- He wanted your childhood to be bad. DID HE SUCCEED?
- He wants any romance in your life to be meaningless to you. IS IT?
- He wants your family to live in chaos. IS HE SUCCEEDING?
- He wants you to hate your spouse. DO YOU?
- He wants you to be a father, but not a dad. DO YOU TAKE TIME FOR YOUR KIDS?
- He wants your children to rebel. HAVE THEY?
- He wants your marriage to fail. HAS IT?
- He wants you to fail in business. ARE YOU STRUGGLING?
- He wants you to roam from church to church. ARE YOU STABLE?

❦ If you're gonna be a Christian, he wants you to have only Pocketknife-sized not Sword-sized Faith. HOW MUCH FAITH DO YOU HAVE?

Satan's frontal attack will be flanked by additional temptations and while your rear is unguarded, he'll attack from that direction too. Another full-scale assault is coming! So, suit up and put on the whole armor of God!

Ephesians 6:13-17 does not ask us to put on God's armor, it DEMANDS that we do:

13Wherefore take unto you the whole armour of God, that ye may be able to withstand in the evil day, and having done all, to stand.

14Stand therefore, having your loins girt about with truth, and having on the breastplate of righteousness;

15And your feet shod with the preparation of the Gospel of peace;

16Above all, taking the shield of faith, wherewith ye shall be able to quench all the fiery darts of the wicked.

17And take the helmet of salvation, and the sword of the Spirit, which is the Word of God.

These Scriptures say you must have your feet shod with the preparation of the Gospel. Therefore, obey 2 Timothy 2:15 and, *Study to shew thyself approved unto God, a workman that needeth not to be ashamed, rightly dividing the Word of truth.* Otherwise, the enemy can knock your feet right out from under you.

> If preparation is your foundation, your dedication will turn to courage, then execution will become your mission and victory will be your reward!

There is another thing I would add to the armor. I think kneepads are essential, too. I know kneepads are not mentioned in the Bible, but since Hellfighters are praying men, its time for our prayers to avail much. James 5:16b promises us that *The effectual fervent prayer of a righteous man availeth much.* So, bend your knee, brother, and pray like you've never prayed before. Satan is going to attack you again and again and again. You will not know when or where, so you better be ready.

When the onslaught of Satan's rampage begins, these are some of the battles you will have to wage. Of course, Satan will use deceit at first to contradict God's truths. Here's what <u>that old liar</u> says about a few of the things God considers to be precious:

▼ "OBEDIENCE is not cool! Disobedience shows individuality! Go ahead, do it your way!"
▼ "Kids, forget about this CHASTITY thing! It's not important to anyone anymore."
▼ "You don't need to waste anymore time STUDYING YOUR BIBLE! It's just a bunch of old wives' tales."
▼ "And that PRAYING thing! Haven't you heard? … God's deaf!"

If Satan fails to deceive you with these lies, and he better since you're a Hellfighter, then he will throw a deluge of enticements at you, all at one time.

Prior to this, your battles have primarily come through worldly temptations that appear obvious to many. Now, however, Satan will try a sly approach that will shockingly go unnoticed by most. He will attempt to infiltrate your home and family activities!

His enticements will come through TV, movies, music, Internet, magazines and acquaintances.

How can you stop his onslaught against you? How can you defeat Satan at his own game? For starters, comply with the following tactics proven to hit Satan where it hurts as he attacks you and your family via the media:

- TV – Turn off your TV! Unhook the cable or the antenna and watch only clean wholesome videos or DVDs. Better still, throw the TV in the garbage. This will help keep that rascal out of your home.

- MOVIES – If it isn't G rated, don't go see it! If you do go see a PG rated movie and the cussing starts, get up and walk out! Let the world see you stand for something.

Before you and your family members go to the theater to see a movie, visit www.pluggedinonline.com to get a Christian review on the film.

- MUSIC – The lyrics of secular music today are no longer love sonnets. They're filled with profanity; they promote hate, violence, sex, drugs, murder and rape. Everything that is vile is being sent over our airwaves. Turn this filth off! Listen to music and programming that will exhort Christ in your daily walk and educate you in a positive sense. Tune into American Family Radio, K-LOVE or some other Christian station.

- INTERNET – Take it out of your home if you can't stand the temptation! If you must have access to the web in your home, the least you can do to protect yourself and your innocent children is install an Internet filter on your computer. That and discipline will do the trick.

- MAGAZINES – Most every newsstand and convenience store has *Playboy, Penthouse, Hustler* and a multitude of similar pornographic magazines for sale. Hopefully, you won't have any problem refraining from purchasing one of these; however, you no longer have to purchase them to view pornography in your home. It will be sent to your door free of charge via mail order catalogs.

♥ MAIL ORDER CATALOGS – Don't think your kids aren't getting an eye full. Victoria's Secret, Undergear, Abercrombie & Fitch, Venus Swimwear and other similar apparel companies provide sensuality and near nudity in most all their catalogs. For the immature mind of a child, this soft-core porn is just as detrimental as full blown, hard-core porn is to adults.

If nasty catalogs come to your home, throw them in the garbage. Then write the sender and ask them to take your name off their mailing list. Tell them why you don't want their catalog sent to your home anymore. Include a Gospel tract or New Testament when you write them.

♥ IPODS & CELL PHONES – Porn films have been around since the early 1900s, however, for many years they were only shown in sleaze joints and at stag parties. In the 1970s, however, HBO and Cinemax ushered these unwanted guests right into our homes. In 1989, porn became an unwanted guest not only in our homes, but also in the workplace, classroom and every other place imaginable via the technological advancement known as the World Wide Web.

Today, everything nasty and damaging to the minds of our children is being made available by the slut merchants via iPods and cell phones! No longer do the screens of our children's cell phones display just text messages and innocent photos of their friends. Now, porn is as accessible as the weather. Every perverted act of sex imaginable can be seen by children of any age on their cell phones and iPods and Mom and Dad will never know!

What can be done to fight Satan in this despicable assault against our families? It's up to parents to prevent children from accessing mobile porn. Contact your service provider to find out how you can block adult sites from being accessed from ALL your family members' phones. And remember, pornographic images can also be sent to phones via text messaging. Get involved! Warn your kids about the dangers of pornography!

● FRIENDS – If the people you hang around with don't have the same desire to serve God with all their hearts, souls and minds as you do… then, convert them to a Hellfighter's way of thinking or

Faith Believing... gives us eternal life with Christ.

Faith Exercised... gives eternal life to others.

Faith Unwaivering... gives victory over Satan.

dump them and make new friends! Matthew 22:37 says, ...*Thou shalt love the Lord thy God with all thy heart, and with all thy soul, and with all thy mind.* 1 Corinthians 15:33b (NKJV) also gives us a straightforward warning when it says, *"Evil company corrupts good habits."*

TAKE A STAND! Be bold and courageous! If we're going to tear the devil's strongholds down, we must ATTACK not just defend! 2 Corinthians 10:4 encourages us to do just that, *For the weapons of our warfare are not carnal, but mighty through God to the pulling down of strongholds.*

Life is a test.
If you fail, it's hell!

NO WEAPON FORMED AGAINST YOU SHALL PROSPER, ...SAYS THE LORD.

ISAIAH 54:17 (NKJV)

CHAPTER 8

The Hellfighter's Sword of Victory

Have you achieved the ultimate victory in Jesus? Not yet! That comes after you die. But, until then we must defend our faith as if each day were to be our last. Romans 8:37b assures us that we will be victorious because ...*we are more than conquerors through Him that loved us.*

So, until your date with destiny comes, share what you've learned with others! You and your fellow Hellfighters can change the face of

Christendom and set Satan's progress back 50 years! If, you'll just tell others what you know!

People all around you are in the throws of battle, and it's up to you to tell them that Satan is defeatable! It's up to you to tell them that he's not invincible like the world wants them to believe. You must tell everyone that only Jesus is invincible! It's up to you to tell all Believers and non-believers about the weapon they must have and utilize effectively in order to defeat Satan – FAITH IN JESUS!

Jesus told His disciples in Matthew 16:18b ...*I will build My church; and the gates of hell shall not prevail against it.* This verse triumphantly means that He and everything He stands for, and upholds, is indestructible and undefeatable. And since He upholds those of us who trust in Him, then we too are undefeatable!

Your Weapon of Faith will prove to be all I've said it to be. But, you are the key to making its power known to the world around you. You must no longer keep silent. You must speak out.

Sir William Wallace died proclaiming the cause he believed in... FREEDOM! Do you have such courage? I sure hope so!

Goliath also died believing in a cause. Was Goliath wrong to die for what he believed? Absolutely not! Goliath's problem was that he had bad information as to what was right and what was wrong.

> No one can make good decisions if they're given bad information. The Bible has reliable information to help everyone make the right decisions.

It is up to you to share the information that you now possess. That's right, if you hoard the wealth of information that you have learned from your study of God's Word and the revelations He has given you during your prayer and Bible study times with Him, you will do mankind a grave injustice and insult the One who died for you. If you fail to tell the lost about Christ then you will be an embarrassment to Him and to all those who gave their lives to defend so great a faith as ours.

David, who killed Goliath, was victorious because the *cause* he believed in was a noble one to set men free from bondage. David was willing to die for what he believed in and you should be too. Paul said in Philippians 1:21, ...*to live is Christ, and to die is gain.* So whether Hellfighters live or die, Hellfighters win!

If your Sword of Committed Faith has grown through your faithfulness and dedication to the Lord Jesus Christ, you now have the privilege to defend that faith with The Hellfighters Sword of Victory! With it you will not only defend yourself against that sorry old deceiver Satan, you will also be able to attack his strongholds.

You no longer have to doubt where your power comes from or who you are solely dependent upon. You no longer have to rely on self, but upon the power of Christ alone to help you motivate others to stand with us and proclaim the mighty truths of the Gospel.

You and I, together with Hellfighters from around the world, must raise our swords of faith, maturity, obedience, defense, commitment and victory and pledge our allegiance to Jesus Christ our Lord. We must lift our voices of encouragement as we exemplify our standards of leadership for the entire world to see. The lost must hear from your lips and mine the resounding cry that has been heralded across the

If you give Satan an inch, he'll become your ruler!

centuries by the apostle John and millions of other soulwinning Hellfighters, *YE MUST BE BORN AGAIN* (John 3:7b).

So com'on, Hellfighter! What are you waiting for—LET'S GO GETTUM!

LIFE IS A TEST.
IF YOU FAIL, IT'S HELL!

...CHOOSE YOU THIS DAY WHOM YOU WILL SERVE... BUT AS FOR ME AND MY HOUSE, WE WILL SERVE THE LORD.

JOSHUA 24:15

CHAPTER 9

Mission Accomplished

K, Bubba, it's show time! It's time to get off your "blessed assurance" and get busy for Jesus!

It's time to let God unleash the power that is within you. Jesus said in John 14:12, *...He that believeth on Me, the works that I do shall he do also; and greater works than these shall he do...*

You may only have Pocketknife-sized Faith right now, but if you will study your Bible and pray, as

> **Seek ye first the kingdom of God, and His righteousness; and all these things shall be added unto you.**
>
> MATTHEW 6:33

you know you should, you will become as awesome a Hellfighter as Satan has ever faced!

I personally believe you've got what it takes! Jesus believed in you enough to die for you and His death provided everything you need to defeat your adversary.

Now, you must exercise your faith in Him. Be excited, be enthusiastic and be vocal! Joshua 6:16b excitedly says, …*Shout; for the LORD hath given you the city.* 1 Chronicles 16:31 (NKJV) announces to all who will hear, *Let the heavens rejoice, and let the earth be glad; and let them say among the nations, "The LORD reigns!"*

Don't let your faith in God remain as small as a pocketknife. Too many Christians already maintain that little tidbit of faith. You need to be an exception to the rule! Your faith needs to be so well grounded, so firm and so steadfast that your

Weapon of Faith becomes so large and powerful that it requires two hands to handle it!

You may be the one who will make an eternal difference in the lives of millions. But, before you can lead millions to Christ, you must first lead one. I believe you can, if you haven't already. All you have to do is be obedient.

Remember: SALVATION is your vehicle, FAITH is your fuel, and GOD'S WORD is your guide. It will take all three to accomplish your mission!

It may take a lifetime to fulfill the purpose God has for you. But when your task on earth is finished, and you enter Heaven through those Pearly Gates, you'll find yourself walking down the Street of Gold beside the Crystal Sea. In your hands will be the magnificent crowns which you have won in your service for King Jesus.

As you savor the thrill of your arrival into Heaven, you'll want to go first to the throne room of God. You'll probably be anxious to enter—I know I will be—and soon you'll recognize that the light of His Glory is beckoning you to come in. Humbly you'll make your way inside and there He will be—Christ Jesus, the One and only Son of God, your Savior, Redeemer and Lord—seated upon His throne!

As you bow down before Him, in worship and adoration, you'll place your crowns of faithful service at His feet and even though there will be no more tears of sadness in Heaven, I believe tears of joy will flow freely down your face. As you are kneeling before Him, He will rise, and ask you to rise also. You'll obey without hesitation. As you rise to your feet, you'll look into His eyes and with great anticipation ask, "How did I do, Lord, how did I do?" Gently He'll place His hands on your shoulders, look into your eyes, and with a smile respond with the words you've longed to hear, *Well done, thou good and faithful servant: thou hast been faithful over a few things, I will make thee ruler over many things: enter thou into the joy of thy lord* (Matthew 25:21).

You will be flooded with the most overwhelming joy and satisfaction you've ever known. Then suddenly that inconceivable moment will be interrupted by a tumultuous roar from outside His throne room. Jesus will walk with you to one of the many windows draped with magnificent fabrics. Asking the Lord what the commotion is all about, He will say, "Why don't you open the curtains, and see for yourself?"

Astonished at the sight of millions of white-robed saints *standing* in God's grand courtyard, applauding, and cheering; again you'll ask, "What's this all about?"

His smile will now be from ear to ear as He replies, "All My servants receive victorious welcomes for a job well done; My Hellfighters, however, receive *standing* ovations!"

As Hellfighters from around the world strive for and look forward to that ultimate moment, we must take advantage of this great privilege that is being afforded us by the King of kings and Lord of lords, which allows us to introduce the lost to Christ. None of us will ever know, this side of Heaven, what impact our lives will have on others. So, let's be busy about the Master's business. The lost are depending on you and me to set them free. So, what are you waiting for, Hellfighter? LET'S GO GETTUM!

WE ARE BOUND
TO THANK GOD
ALWAYS FOR YOU,
BRETHREN…
BECAUSE YOUR
FAITH GROWS
EXCEEDINGLY…

2 THESSALONIANS 1:3A (NKJV)

CHAPTER 10

The Invitation

After reading this book, you should be able to determine what size faith you have. If your faith isn't even the size of a pocketknife, then maybe you aren't even saved. Maybe your faith isn't growing because you don't have anyone to place

Life has many choices. Eternity only has two: Heaven or hell!

your faith in. If that's the case, we need to get you fixed up with Jesus. He's waiting to become your Savior, if you're ready to let Him become your Lord. If you are, please pray the following prayer and experience the joy of perfect peace.

The Sinner's Prayer

Heavenly Father,

I repent of my sins and ask You to forgive me for all I have done wrong. Please save me. I know now that the joy You have for me is everlasting and everything I need I will find in You. I know You will lead me because the Bible says, if I will hide Your Word in my heart I will not sin against Thee. I thank You for Your Word, which will now be a lamp unto my feet, and a light unto my path. I know You will protect me, for You have given Your angels charge concerning me, to protect me in all my ways. Now that I am saved, teach me how to live victoriously for You. I believe You will reveal to me the mysteries of Your Holy Word because of Your promise in Jeremiah 33:3 that says, *Call unto*

Me, and I will answer thee, and shew thee great and mighty things, which thou knowest not. Amen

Sign your name here if you've accepted Jesus, and know for sure that He is now your Savior and you're willing to let Him be your Lord:

> **For to me to live is Christ, and to die is gain.**
> PHILIPPIANS 1:21

_____

Signature

_____

Date

Now, what are YOU waiting for, Hellfighter? LET'S GO GETTUM!

I HAVE FOUGHT A
GOOD FIGHT,
I HAVE FINISHED
MY COURSE,
I HAVE KEPT THE
FAITH.

2 TIMOTHY 4:7

Epilogue

Well, that's it! Or is it? The truth is, your adventure is just beginning! Now that you have full knowledge of the potential you can reach in your service to the King of kings and Lord of lords, you will be held accountable for your decision as to what you will do with that knowledge. The choice is yours.

So, what will the rest of your life be like? Will it be a rewarding adventure into the realm of total commitment as a Hellfighter for Jesus Christ, or will it be a mediocre adventure into the realm of lackadaisical do-nothingness as an average church-goer. The magnitude of your faith will dictate the realm in which you will serve from this point forward.

One path will bring out the best in you, the other the worst. One will cause Satan to tremble in his boots, the other will expose you to the destructive forces that Satan wants to hurl against you. One will allow you to do great things for God, the other will let you rest on your laurels and do absolutely nothing and waste away. One will allow you to bring honor and glory to God, the other will cause you to blaspheme His Holy Name.

What's it gonna be? Will you be a committed warrior for our great God Jehovah, or will you be a pawn in the hands of the blasphemous ruler of hell?

You will either raise your sword against Satan as a Hellfighter or you will lay it at his feet like most church-goers and live a defeated life of mediocrity. THE CHOICE IS YOURS!

A Hellfighter's Pledge

I, the undersigned,
do solemnly swear that I
have pledged my allegiance
to the Lamb of God.
I promise to defend the cause of Christ
and to use the power He has given to me.
I will use my Weapon of Faith
for the good of mankind and I will
do my best to search for and rescue
the perishing. I consider it an honor and
a privilege to be among His league
of extraordinary ladies and gentlemen
for which only the bold will qualify.
I am and always will be a
Hellfighter!

_____

Signature

_____

Date

About the Author

Richard Headrick is a successful businessman whose passion is writing encouraging and thought provoking books for Christians and Christian-wannabes.

See the following pages for a list of products by Richard Headrick.

Richard has written many books, including:

The Well

The Circular Rings of Kansas

Poor Richard's Proverbs

The Treasures of Solomon

A Redneck's Guide to Financial Freedom

Goliath's Fall

America's Churches through the Eyes of a Bum

Hellfighters Operations Manual 1:
The Call of a Hellfighter

Hellfighters Operations Manual 2:
The Commission of a Hellfighter

The Enemy of Heaven

The Seven Churches

My Other Little Book on The Seven Churches

Love Letters from a King

God, If We're the Best You've Got, You're in Big Trouble

Why Everybody Needs Jesus

Richard has also written Gospel tracts, including:

Richard the Rhino Man
Hellfighters
Have a Great Day!
Orangevestitis
Will Someone Plant a Tree for You?
Something Special
Guardian Angels
Is Hell Right for You?
There's Only One Thing Better Than a Hummer
In the Company of Fish
The War Wagon
Nickel Tissue
The World is Ablaze
Keeping Christ in Christmas
I'm Here for the Party!
SATAN SUCKS

Some books and tracts are out of print, but may still be available through various sources. Go to www.hellfighters.org or send us an e-mail to info@hellfighters.org to order these books and other items that are available. If we've got it in stock, then you've got it. If we don't have it, we'll tell you who may have it and where you might be able to get it. If nobody has 'em, it means you've waited too late and missed out.

It's OK to miss out on these books, but don't mess around and miss out on Heaven.

Other Hellfighter Productions
Keeping Christ in Christmas – audio CD
Christians Still Die – DVD
Last Ounce of Courage - DVD

Heaven's sweet, Hell's hot. You're going to one, Ready or not!

HELLFIGHTER PUBLICATIONS
One Freedom Square
Laurel, MS 39440-3367
601-649-HOPE (4673)
www.hellfighters.org
info@hellfighters.org

To be continued...

Now that you've read The Conflict of a Hellfighter, have you committed your life to serving Jesus Christ boldly and courageously? Are you ready to do battle with the enemy by wielding your Hellfighter's Sword of Victory? If so, I commission you, my fellow Hellfighter, into The Lord's Army! Keep an eye out for the next Hellfighters Operations Manual, you won't want to miss it! Now... what are you waiting for? Let's Go Gettum!

Read On!

[1] London School of Economics, January 2002

[2] Top Ten Reviews, 2007 Internet Pornography Statistics, accessed at http://internet-filter-review.toptenreviews.com/internet-pornography-statistics.html on October 14, 2007.

Glossary of Terms

Accepting Jesus – Denouncing Satan and placing one's trust in Jesus Christ.

Believer in Jesus Christ – A person who has denounced Satan and placed his trust in the Son of God.

Corporate Worship – The assembling of Believers in an established setting such as the church house or worship center.

Giver of Eternal Security – God.

Guidebook to Victorious Living – The Bible.

His Holy Word – The Bible.

Mediocre Christian – A born again Believer who does just enough for Jesus to appear righteous.

Satan's Deceptive Practices – The art of getting a person to believe that wrong is right and bad is good.

Satan's Seductive Pleasures – Any sinful act of wrongdoing that satisfies the flesh.

Sho-Nuf Believer – "Sho-nuf" is slang for "sure enough."

Skin His Hide – Win a fight.

Wailing and Gnashing of Teeth - Suffering and anguish in its worse state.

Whole Armor of God –The only protection, specified by God, that a person has against the forces of evil. The details of each piece of the armor is found in Ephesians 6:11-17.